Park Song

Ron Walker

Illustrated by J.K. Dooley

*Personal Encounters with the Natural World
in Custer State Park*

Big Water Press | Lake of the Ozarks

Copyright © 2023 by **Ron Walker**

All rights reserved. No part of this publication may be reproduced, distributed or transmitted in any form or by any means, without prior written permission.

Ron Walker/Big Water Press
2399 Twin Rivers Point
Camdenton, MO 65020
www.bigwaterpress.com

Book Layout © 2017 BookDesignTemplates.com

Park Song/ Ron Walker. -- 1st ed.
ISBN 978-1-7364200-1-0

This book is dedicated to my grandchildren: Brinna, Emma, Hadley, Owen, Cienna, Quinn, Reid, Benaiah, Frankie, Nora, and Elizabeth

Contents

Chapter 1. Bison Journey 1
Chapter 2. The Work of Fire 35
Chapter 3. The Human Story 45
Chapter 4. Horses 53
Chapter 5. Tapestry 69

Introduction

Custer State Park occupies over 110 square miles and extends from the mountain heights of Sylvan Lake to the prairie interface along the south-eastern edge of the Black Hills of South Dakota. The park's forestlands cover about 50,000 acres and its rangelands occupy about 21,000 acres. The park actively manages its natural resources. Park officials shape the density of the forest and protect its health; they affect the grazing pressures and patterns of wildlife using the rangelands; they regulate the size of wildlife populations; they suppress destructive wildfires, yet at the same time apply fire to the landscape in beneficial ways. Park officials harvest the natural production of its various landscapes by selling timber, harvesting wildlife and regulating the size and composition of the bison herd through hunting seasons and live animal sales. When I worked there, the revenues resulting from these activities were invested back into the operation of the park to benefit South Dakota citizens because of its limited use of state tax revenues. The park operated as a financially self-supporting division of South Dakota Game, Fish and Parks until 2004, when it merged with the Division of Parks and Recreation.

The park hosts nearly two million visitors each year, 80% of which are from outside South Dakota, and its wildlife-abundant acres have enriched the lives of generations of visitors. Custer State Park is one of the great places in America. Its resource management enhances a great visitor experience by releasing the diversity and productivity of the land base for all to enjoy.

The '80s and '90s were unfriendly times for resource management. This tough environment primarily manifested itself at the federal level. Although the park was insulated from that adversarial environmental politic by virtue of it being a state government operation, that insulation was not very secure.

The US Forest Service (USFS) was regularly in court answering litigation from various environmental groups seeking to obstruct timber sales. The National Park Service (NPS) was embroiled in controversy over bison diseases as they potentially affected ag economies of entire states. Environmentalism took on a seemingly religious-like expression, and things like diseased bison and hawks and yellow-bark pine trees became weapons in the fight against the people managing natural resources. The fervor of the battle ran high in the '80s and '90s.

With the park bounded on two sides by the USFS, and on the third side by the NPS, and with the park having such a high public profile in the Black Hills, we needed a firm foundation upon which to build an enduring resource management program. I fielded questions by some in Game, Fish and Parks (GF&P) as to why we didn't follow the provisions in the National Environmental Protection Act (NEPA). NEPA was established government policy. They thought it would be the prudent thing to do but didn't realize how NEPA was being used to litigate against all kinds of wildlife and forest management practices such as timber sales and hunting seasons. The park needed to replace NEPA style management with a "South Dakota friendly" long term management plan that would enjoy the favor of GF&P and the South Dakota court system.

During the summer of 1992, I attended a Holistic Resource Management (HRM) school in Nebraska. HRM is used as a planning system for private ranches in the West. I appreciated how HRM integrated the various management disciplines into a cohesive decision-making model and used it to structure the park's new resource management plan (RMP). It would be a weave of four management disciplines – forest, range, wildlife and fire management – over three landscape types – forestland, rangeland, and open water systems.

Using an HRM-style approach, Bill Hill (timber forester), Dick Sparks (fire forester), Gary Brundige (wildlife biologist) and I took a year off from timber sales, prescribed burning, and other resource work in the park in order to write a new, comprehensive RMP that would operate with a consensus of stakeholders on how natural resource management would look for the next 15 years (1995-2010) in Custer State Park. We brought in a variety of stakeholders as a moderated focus group to consider and review plan elements. In our planning strategy, stakeholders as disparate and adversarial as the Sierra Club and local sawmills had to talk to each other rather than about each other. We wrote the plan, made revisions, and presented it in meetings at ten different locations across the state. The Game Fish and Parks Commission formally adopted it in 1995.

As an end note to the uniqueness of our management approach, the U.S. Department of State sent us a young resource manager named Alfred Byugama from Tanzania in the summer of 1995. The State Department sought another park with a similar management model to Ngorongoro Conservation Area (a world heritage site) and the closest thing they could find was Custer State Park. We received him and gave him a week-long tour of our various management activities. He even walked in on a timber sale auction and so shocked the bidders that the auction came to an unexpected conclusion. I'm sure we lost a little bid premium, but I didn't care. Alfred was a pleasure to have around for the week. The thing that impressed me about Alfred's visit was there were no other parks in the US at that time with a management model like Custer State Park. We were truly one of a kind with a well-supported pro-management approach toward natural resources.

The Custer State Park RMP was a big deal. We were challenged only one time over a timber sale in the Sylvan Lake area but had the solid support of the GF&P commission. The RMP stabilized resource management work in the park for the long term by keeping us out of the arena of conflict.

My name is Ron Walker. I worked in the park from 1979-2005 as the manager of the Resource Program which included timber, range, wildlife, fire, and bison management. I offer to you an insider's view of what it was like to work with the precious natural resources of Custer State Park through a series of snapshots. Travel with me through the sights and sounds and smells of my experience in a mixture of prose and poetry, much of it written prior to 2005. I trust my own song about this special place will strike a warm chord in your heart as well.

Chapter 1. Bison Journey

Bison are iconic to Custer State Park. My earliest memory of the park, as a young boy, was of a buffalo next to our Minnesota car, and my mother refusing to roll down the window because he was so close. Little did I know that, many years later, these animals would come to play such a large part of my life for close to three decades. A significant part of my work in the park took on the rhythm of the herd. It was that natural rhythm that determined our activities; it ebbed and flowed, at times with intensity and at times with easiness.

The mid-July through August breeding season is a time of brutal, violent, and sometimes fatal combat. All the herd bulls assemble with the cow-calf herd for the age-old right to breed the cows. Indeed, it is the only time of year we can census them because, other than the breeding season, they live independent and sometimes solitary lives. The following are some impressions of those seasons. Journey with me through the annual cycle of bison life in the park.

Dust rolling upward
Twin fleering nostrils scenting,
Bold growling challenge,
Red rimmed eyes barely seeing,
Thunder echoes deep within.

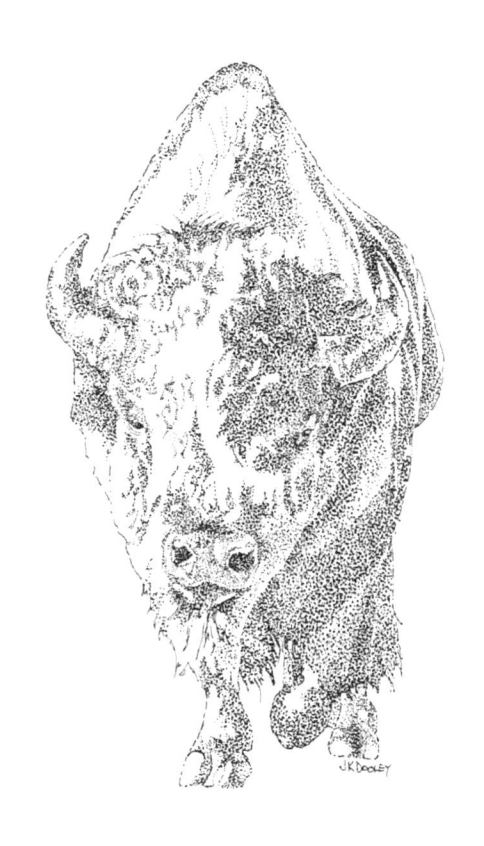

An Old Bull's Ballad

    Eight summers he stood the combat test
    From the springtime he turned two.
    That he still rumbled would attest
    He'd fought, survived, and killed a few.
    Many faced him, most withdrew,
    When hormones flowed with summer light,
    When bulls and cows made rendezvous,
    He was driven to roar and bellow and fight.

Former bull partners with vigor detested
His tending the cows they'd rather pursue.
He pissed and pawed as they protested,
determined to leave his residue
in red calves – his genetic brew.
Prairie moon, hot summer night
Cows to be bred, duty to do
He was driven to roar and bellow and fight.

An old bull now, a thunder chest.
Age has slowed his battle review.
Took horns in his neck this last contest,
Badly hurt without a clue
That this last fight would be adieu
to sun, grass, heat and dim twilight.
He only knew there were cows in view
And it drove him to roar and bellow and fight.

His bones grace prairie avenue;
Memory echoes his ancient sight.
Younger bulls from his ancient hue
are driven to roar and bellow and fight.

August Weary

He moves his feet so very slow
a one-ton body, beat and sore.
He answered hormone's call to show
himself and make his roar
as father did, who'd gone before
to battle, wage a war and breed
the cows. He could not ignore
the inner drive to leave his seed.

The long beard swinging to and fro
Bruised joints crying at his core.
Big head sweeping, hanging low.
For him the breeding season's o'er
even though the cows were more.
He cannot match the young bull's speed.
His presence there they now deplore
in the drive to leave their seed.

The years of youth seem long ago.
Fall-winter-spring might health restore.
Winter snows o'er him will flow
and o'er a hundred days he'll snore
away the time to heal the gore
of battle where others did the deed
as he- in the time of his encore
in the drive to leave his seed.

The end is knocking at his door
and others o'er him will succeed.
He's done time in the breeding corps

Preparations for the fall roundup begin in September. The breeding season bruises along until September and intertwines with the first gather. It's a time for cross-country buffalo drives and sweaty horses, crisp fall mornings and hot afternoons, and long days in the saddle. The green of summer begins to give way to the brilliant tones of autumn. The musty smell of bison mingles with the sweet smell of horse flesh. Big bunches of cows, calves, young bulls, and yearlings are moved south, pushed by pushing horses. "You can push the cows and yearlings, but you'd best leave the tending bulls alone."

Cut bank trail, creek bed
at the east end of French Creek
cows, bulls up and o'er
tending bulls won't be denied
thunder joins with lightning strike.

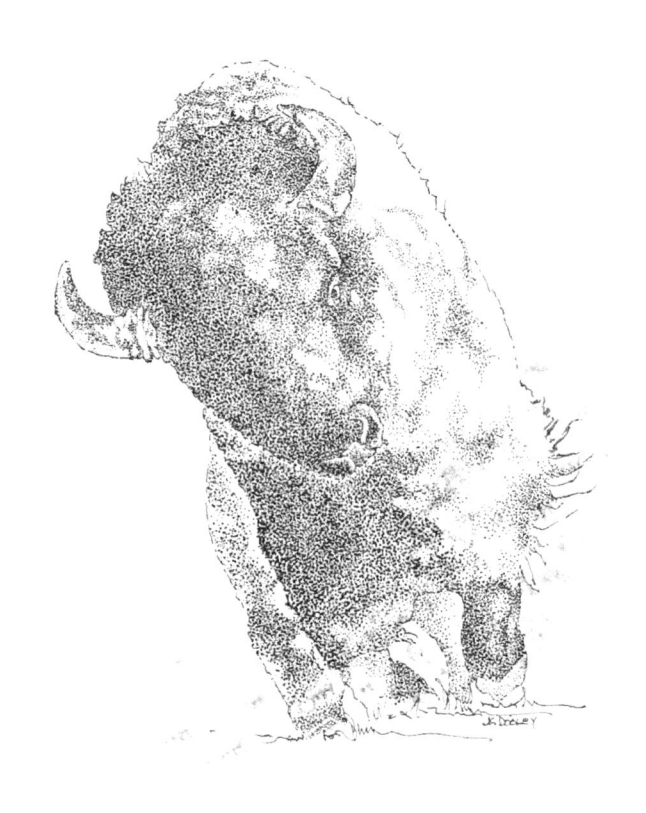

It happened in a hot searing flash on a mid-September day. We had been moving buffalo south in preparation for the roundup. That day I was riding Buddy, an appaloosa gelding, my old herdsman Vern Ekstrom's regular ride. Vern had died the summer before in the Bighorns, in a riding accident. A small group of riders and I had a herd of about 200 moving past French Creek along the east side. They had cleared the bottom, and I followed, ascending the game trail up the cut bank. Midway, the old bull came roaring back over the cut bank rim, head down, all business. Spinning, trying to get out of his way, Buddy and I were blocked by another horse, then shoved atop that horse by the bull. Buddy had a badly bleeding back leg from a heavy blunt horn rammed home like a Roman sword, up to the hilt. As suddenly as the bull appeared, he was gone only to strike again. Bill Hill's mare wasn't so lucky, ambushed from behind, three hard thrusts into the belly, stomach on the ground. She died. "You can push the cows and yearlings but beware of old tending bulls."

We Are Many

"We are many; many strong calves,
Moving, always moving; eating, always eating.
Hot summer, dusty, grass getting shorter.
They come and bother us, push us and we sometimes fight back;
Don't like being pushed.
Many disappear when the grass turns gold and the cold winds blow
Somehow, there's always enough grass.
Moving, eating, resting; moving eating resting.
We like it here; it's our home.
Many have gone before, many will follow.
We are many."

Prior to 2005, the annual fall roundup took place over two days, Sunday and Monday. About 60 riders participated with us in the event. On Sunday, we drove the herd to the east half of the R&D pasture, the park's southernmost pasture unit, where we let them rest overnight. Our objective the second day was to put the herd in the corrals. On Monday, we drove the herd east from where they were left the day before, then turned them north into a trap and finally turned them west into the corrals. In the early 1990s State Tourism began to promote the event on a national scale, resulting in massive crowds of 10-20 thousand people witnessing the final day of the roundup. These were the logistics and plans and the general workings of the roundup.

But the event had a personality and a psyche. You could sense it from sixty invited horses tied to their trailers, a hundred twenty-four hooves pawing and stomping. You could sense it at the early-morning briefings for those sixty riders as we went over team routes and timing and safety; that psyche showing in the quiet attentive faces of those normally over-confident cowboys. It showed in the presence of the governor and his staff. It showed in the assembled teams as we left first from Cow Camp and then, the next day, out the back way from the corrals toward each team's respective assignment. It showed in me as Red and I climbed the long escarpment to the edge of Hay Flats on Monday morning, radio in hand to direct the initial movements of the horseback teams. The psyche of the unfolding event was nervous and fast and wild and bold and big. Join with me in the following two poems and experience the flavor of the event.

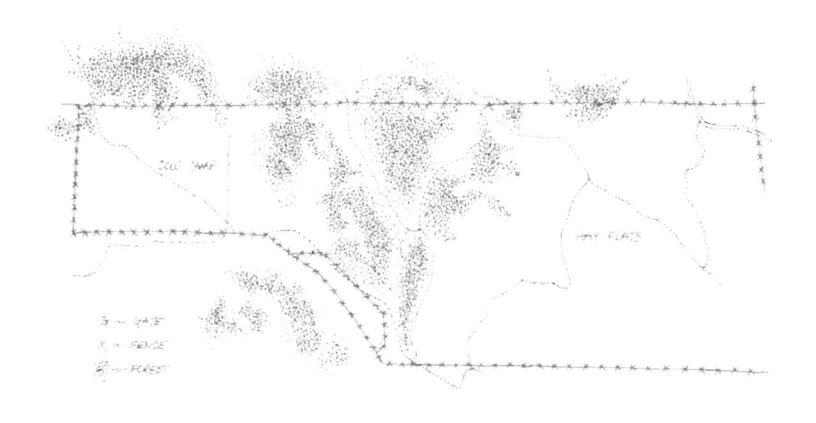

Sunday

>The herd is finally on the mesa,
>Fifteen hundred head of bison.
>Three miles sweaty horses chased 'em
>Through trees, steep hills, rocks and spaces
>To leave now herd and long horizon.
>
>We pause now– horse and buffalo,
>The ancient scene a full eyed feast
>witnessing a past forgotten;
>timeless dance of man and beast.
>
>A dance of hooves and horns and thunder
>Prairie passion, breakneck speed,
>Whips a crackin', surging wonder,
>Horse and bison fast stampede.
>
>
>They rumble past old bronze encampment;

heaving brown backs, fiery steeds.
The great herd surges down escarpment;
flying riders, hot blood horses
race steep slopes with crashing speed.

The brown backs flow like family totem
To the lower bench asunder.
Horsemen race them to the bottom;
cross the creek and through the gates
to wait tomorrow's play with thunder.

A dance of hooves and horns and thunder
Prairie passion, breakneck speed.
Whips a crackin', surging wonder,
Horse and bison fast stampede.

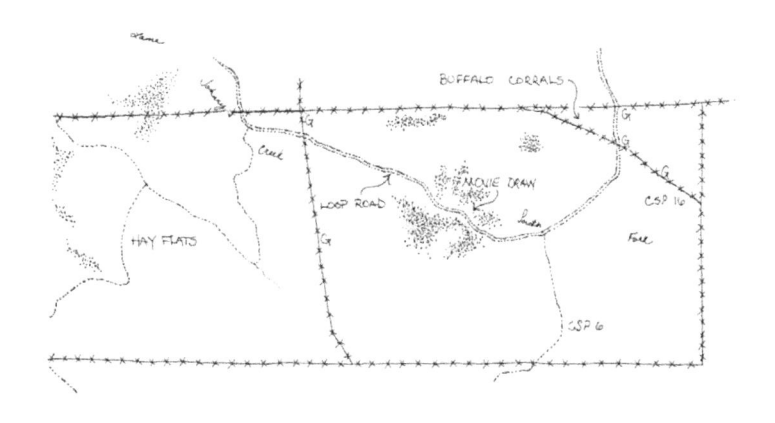

Monday

The dark dawn's laced with white light beams
Red white strobes stretch to horizon.
Thousands come to live the dreams
They gaze into a past forgotten
Witness dance of horse and bison.

"Red team – Lame Johnny
Push and see where they will go
Drive them all eastward
If they come up to Hay Flats
Blue team will take them eastward."

"White team on north fence
Clear bison toward the bottom.
Red team on creek bed
Will catch them as they go east
Down the Lame Johnny Creek bed."

"Let them settle down.
Blue team to the east corner,
Turn them toward the north;
Push them past Lame Johnny
Into the trap east of corrals."

Totem flow with hoofbeat dust clouds
Creatures rumble toward the gap
Bison thrill assembled watch crowds
History steps from past to present
Rushing like a thunderclap.

"Red, blue white as one
Must now ride as one big team
Wheel them to the west
Across the Wildlife Loop Road
Through two sets of double gates."

Through the big gate final courses
Riders form a common line
Herd surges from the foam flecked horses
Heaving brown backs cross the blacktop
Scene fades to the mists of time.

The events following the roundup involve many hours at the corrals with predetermined sorting plans, vaccination schedules, branding, weighing and tagging. All that work leads to the annual fall auction, the third Saturday in November, where normally 350 head are sold through live auction. The revenues from the auction are used to operate the park.

The chute work which followed corralling the herd was a noisy, moving picture of animals being shuffled through the chutes, smoke of burning hair from branding, and multiple sorts, weighing, testing, vaccinations and blood draws.

It required about 60 volunteers plus CSP staff to man the corrals at peak operation. For many volunteers and seasonals, the corral work was a reward at the end of a long summer's tourist season. They were our gate runners, opening and closing the gates as buffalo passed through to the next station. I deliberately stayed away from a hydraulic head chute because I needed the jobs for the volunteers.

For many years we handled the herd twice, in the fall and the winter. The winter handling was a far lower profile event and was done to prepare animals sold separately from the auction. Staffing the corrals was more difficult in the winter. I used Youth Forestry Camp boys (incarcerated juvenile delinquents) during the Gov. Janklow years, trustees (inmates on supervised work release). That labor source had its own special challenges. Trustees were rough and often had attitude.

One winter day, a trustee running a swing gate was being too rough with his prod stick, and after I chastened him he stuck his stick out and sneered, "Get this!" Without thinking I swung my bull whip at the stick and as the end of the whip wrapped several times around the stick it cracked loudly. His sneer turned to shock as he dropped the stick. He ceased being a problem.

My goal with corral work was to process the herd in two days, and the sale adults on the third day. I felt like we were sitting on a keg of explosives with 1,500 penned buffalo, and the faster we could get the herd through, the better. It made me a bit of a slave driver. Breaks and lunches ended with, "Park crew, get back to work."

One time we were testing calves prior to the auction and a late fall storm was coming down Lame Johnny Road. We worked the calves at a fever clip, but as we were on the last 10 of 200 head, the storm hit the corrals. Ice water filled my ears as we finished the last one.

I moved from place to place as we processed the herd through the corrals, making sure the crew kept on top of things, and dealing with issues as they arose. Occasionally an animal went down and had to be field dressed. We tried to cut back as many old bulls as we could in the gather, but we never got rid of them all. They were dangerous. I remember an old bull by a gate in a large pen, filled with other buffalo. I swung the gate open and shut until I got the old boy's attention. He finally got the idea he could get out, and I accommodated him. He walked through a parking lot full of cars as I bid him a "good day."

Our vaccination schedule required six weeks to complete. It included testing for brucellosis and tuberculosis and results had to be returned by the time of the auction in Novembers. I failed to complete the testing schedule one time; I trusted the mail. Lesson learned, I personally drove samples to Pierre after that, and to Brookings when necessary. Incomplete testing meant we couldn't ship animals after the auction.

Occasionally we would fail to catch an animal in the head chute. When that happened, we would have to send it back through the sale ring, and it would make a second trip through the chutes. I would often be in the sale ring to recycle missed animals. Once a cow turned on me and came after me. I grabbed the hair between her horns and stiff armed her as she pushed me across the sale ring, hooking and snorting. I was planning how to get away from her when she backed me up to the sale ring fence, but she pulled away before that happened. The people on the catwalk grew very quiet. I still have a white scar on my forearm where she poked me with a horn.

Calves were orphaned when we sorted out their mothers for sale. They would try to get back to their mothers on the other side of the fence. On several occasions we gathered these calves to put with the sale calves, which we had deliberately shorted to make room for the expected orphaned calves.

Dust was always a problem. I put gravel and mag water in the heavily trafficked areas. Trying to move animals when you could only see ten feet was a thrill, to say the least. I do not recommend it.

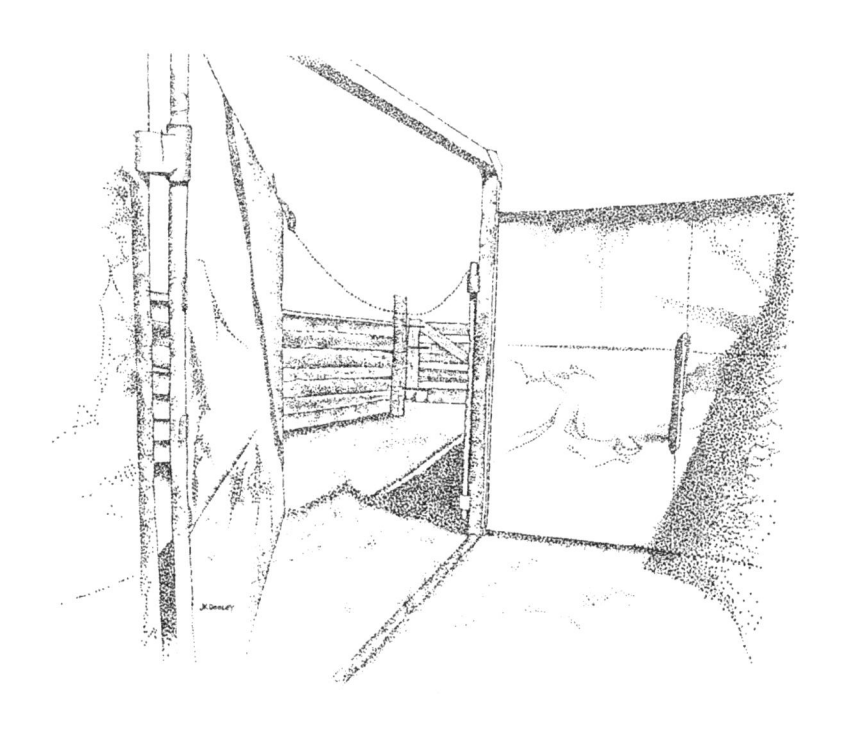

Loadin' Out on Auction Day

    Loadin' out on auction day
    To empty out the pens;
    Yearlins' down the alley way
    and backfill pens again.
    The auction purchased specimens,
    Six wild yearling mates,
    Destined to be denizens
    Just blowin' past the gates.

On a wild auction Saturday
Six headin' to the tub.
"Lock 'em in now, no horseplay"
Upon that loadout hub.
When all at once the lock did rub
They didn't hesitate
All t'was left were woody stubs,
Buffs bustin' through the gates.

Sortin' cows on our payday,
"The right one in the lane!"
Back-tags our little bit display
And they ain't very plain!
Circlin' cows, am I insane?
"Now don't miscalculate
when she comes on you like a train
Just show her lots of gate."
Oftentimes to my dismay
They show their ornery traits.
'Tis enough to turn you gray
Buffs blowin' past the gates.

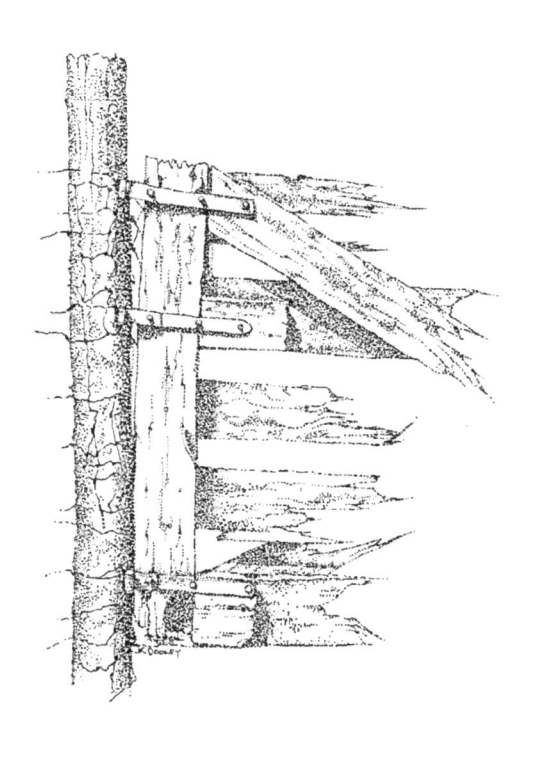

Winter fur sun blond,
descending slope to creek bed,
circling birthing cow,
front legs of calf protruding,
withdrawn and running away.

The fall auction gave way to the bull hunt and winter. Winter can be a grind for us humans, but it is a time of rest for the buffalo herd. Their felt-like under hair allows them to weather the cold and snow without any stress until the temperature drops to -20 degrees Fahrenheit. Day after day the herd fills its collective rumen with winter cured native grasses, and then beds down to chew its collective cud.

Springtime brings about the calving season. I knew there were things we did not know about bison calving. Where did our losses come from? Vern and I decided one spring to spend extensive time on horseback observing calving. He found one calf born dead which was about twice the size of a normal calf. We decided to eliminate our practice of providing a ninety-day supplement in late winter to the cow herd, which, we felt was contributing to oversize calves.

Red was my steady ride. The park acquired him as a ten-year-old. He was a sixteen-hand, thoroughbred-like quarter horse. One day Red and I rode down a wooded hill to the open draw bottom at the Korthaus Place, an old homestead west of Hay Flats. The bottom was full of cows and calves. As we stood there and watched, the herd slowly began to take notice of our presence and leave the area; all except for two cows.

One had just had a calf and waited for it to stand. When it did, they both scampered off to join the rest. The other was in labor. She was up and down several times, and the front legs of the calf protruded. As she lay down again in her labor, a nearly white coyote descended the slope behind her and circled the laboring cow. She eyed him warily. All of a sudden, she drew in her calf's protruding legs, got up and ran off to join the rest. How could she control that? I was stunned. This mother was not about to expose her newborn to the coyote threat alone. She needed the herd. I silently said, "Excuse me," for moving the herd away from her. Bison cows make awesome mothers.

The Rites of Spring

In April, when the grass grows green
at birthing time the coyotes sing.
With calves appearing on the scene
the bison cows do rites of spring
and motherhood's a fearsome thing.
Her care is like His autograph.
She speaks to us of a great king,
He keeps us as she keeps the calf.

A coyote is a death machine
and coyote feasts will bring death's sting.
When springtime sets out fresh cuisine
the bison cows do rites of spring
and motherhood is in full swing.
Her strength is like His photograph
as calves to mothers tightly cling.
He holds us as she holds the calf.

The mother cow stands in between
the joker and her daughterling.
Afterbirth is all he'll glean
when bison cows do rites of spring.
When life's day fades to evening
She feeds him from her carafe
And makes her constant offering.
He feeds us as she feeds the calf.

The trickster would end everything
when bison cows do rites of spring.
Unseen hands on our behalf
guard us as she guards the calf.

Standoff in the forest,
two cows with red calves resting,
five coyotes in a line,
two red slops of afterbirth,
mother cows take calves away.

Victims of our own success

Custer State Park worked as an operationally self-supporting Division of Game Fish and Parks until 2004. All but one year of my 26-year tenure at the park was under this self-supporting business model. Our income streams were timber sales, bison sales, and tourism, with a minimal amount coming from the resort complexes. We often had to adjust our planned spending when the income streams deviated from those used to construct out budget. I was once asked to get operations on a timber sale started faster than the submitted operating plan so we could meet up-coming payroll demands.

One time I told tourism officials that my goal was to sell a million dollars' worth of buffalo from the park in one year. We did that in 1998, actually $1.2 million with all live sales and hunts combined. We turned out to be victims of our own success. When Governor Janklow saw those impressive revenue figures, he said that we no longer needed any state support and withdrew state funding from two contracted water and sewer projects costing over a million dollars each. Paying off these projects collapsed our revolving fund from which we never recovered.

When the bison market collapsed in 2002, the financial pressures seemed insurmountable, and negotiations began to surrender sovereignty of the Division of Custer State Park and become another park in the state park system, run by the Division of Parks and Recreation. The Division of Custer State Park, which had been equal in the organization of Game Fish and Parks to the Division of Wildlife and the Division of Parks and Recreation, was to be no more. The self-supporting business model under which the park had operated for 85 years came to an end. It was a sad day for me to have to give up that self-supporting business model. It meant a loss of freedom that we had so long enjoyed, and another layer of bureaucracy under which we would now operate. Promises made that Custer would become its own subdivision of Parks and Recreation were never realized. I felt manipulated and somehow responsible for the park's demise, much as a child feels responsible for his parents' divorce.

Politics of bison

Brucellosis is a blood born disease in bovids causing abortions and threatening the cattle industry. Brucellosis in bison is the same disease and was a continuing National Park Service (NPS) controversy, especially in Yellowstone National Park (YNP). Wind Cave National Park's (WCNP) approach to brucellosis in their bison herd was restricted so as not to compromise YNP's hands off approach. Only a fence line separated CSP's southern boundary from WCNP. Since CSP was heavily dependent on revenues from the annual bison sale, and since a brucellosis reactor in the park's sale stock would effectively cancel the annual sale, the continuing presence of brucellosis in the Wind Cave herd presented a real danger to the financial stability of Custer State Park.

In the spring of 1983, a most unusual meeting took place. It was early in the Reagan administration, and James Watt was the secretary of interior. South Dakota governor Bill Janklow approached Watt with a possible solution; CSP would absorb WCNP into its operation. This kind of outside-the-box thinking had the potential to cause a significant seismic disturbance in the world of the National Park Service.

I drove to the Hot Springs airport on a spring morning to pick up Warren Jackson, director of CSP, and Doug Hofer, director of Parks and Recreation. We drove to the WCNP headquarters to meet with its superintendent and his staff to discuss the details of such a takeover. It was a surprisingly cordial meeting, given the potential of the NPS losing a national park to a state. We were treated with respect and not hostility. At the end of the day, after reviewing budgets and staffing and operating details, the two state directors recommended not to proceed. I think Hofer and Jackson were a bit intimidated by the NPS. After that meeting, WCNP began to clean up the brucellosis in its bison herd. I think the NPS was a bit intimidated by Governor Janklow.

Some years later, the National Park Service contracted with Dr. James Durr of Texas A&M to evaluate the level of bovine genetic introgression in its various bison herds. (Genetics introduced into the herd's genetic profile due to past crossbreeding events with domestic cattle) I was astonished to learn that the bison in Wind Cave National Park were completely free of any bovine genes, although the Custer State Park herd had a trace of bovine introgression in its genetic profile. This would mean that the "pure" bison herd in Wind Cave would have to somehow be protected from the "impure" herd in Custer State Park.

I was suspicious because I knew some of the history of the two herds. Wind Cave had an agreement with CSP during the 1950s to roll back their north fence for a month each year and attempt to drive some of their bison north in order to reduce their herd numbers. The fence was occasionally breached, as most fences are, during the '80s and '90s. Bulls occasionally walked cattle guards. Previous genetic research showed the herd profiles to be nearly identical. However, in accordance with this newly acquired research, WCNP developed a policy that required shooting any branded CSP bison that became mixed with the Wind Cave herd, lest they corrupt what they surmised was their pristine gene pool. We began receiving calls from WCNP on June 8, 2004. They had shot one of our bulls, a 6-year-old. On July 14 they called with the news they had killed two more bulls, an 8 and 9-year-old. (They had given us one hour to remove them.) On August 16 they called and said there was a CSP cow mixed with their herd, and that we had one day to remove her. Chad Kremer, our herdsman, and I gathered our normal volunteer horseback riders. We tried mightily, but at the end of the day, failed to catch and remove her. The next day she was shot and killed. The WCNP policy was based on what I would come to know confidentially, was flawed research; the genetic profiles were indeed identical, and my suspicion of politicized research was justified.

Wandering bulls

I received a call from Tom LeFaive, the CSP maintenance supervisor, on the Friday after Thanksgiving one year; he asked me if I'd been listening to the radio. The DJ said there was an old bull working his way up Greyhound Gulch and would soon be in Keystone. I called Fred Matthews, my original herdsman, and together we went to look for him. The old bull was near the top of the drainage, camped out by an old trailer and some hay bales piled by a rope corral. Fred and I had already decided there would be no live return for this bull. He was too old, too ornery, too far away, and in too remote and rough country.

Fred and I both exited the pickup with our park issued 30-06 rifles. The bull gave neither of us a side shot as he began to walk away from us, but we both were trying to angle a killing shot to the axis joint behind the skull. Fred shot three times; I shot three times; the bull continued his walk up the gulch. I climbed the ridge next to the road and ran to catch up with him through knee-deep snow, and when I did, I was so winded that I could not shoot. I rested briefly, caught up again a bit more collected, and delivered a bullet to his ear, which collapsed him in the snow.

Fred pulled up behind him in his pickup. The bull jumped up again. I shot him once more in the ear and killed him. Those old bulls are so tough! He absorbed seven shots toward the joint at the base of his skull from two guys who knew where to shoot. We took him into the A&K Market in Custer that Friday evening. Our good friend Art Richardson never turned us down to salvage one of these bulls.

Another year, during the summer, we had two young bulls escape our north perimeter fence, and they began showing up on Highway 40 east of Keystone. Although I traveled the road a number of times, I had yet to see them. On a summer Saturday, I thought I would try it again. As I began to travel Highway 40, I saw a man with a rifle slung over his shoulder and thought it prudent to talk with him.

"*Have you seen our two bulls?*"

"*Not yet, but they're not going to get me and my family!*"

I asked him to ride with me. My intention had been to shag these two young bulls back to the park. We found some tracks and followed them to the north rim of Greyhound Gulch.

Duane Webster, one of the park's law enforcement officers, had also been out and we communicated by radio.

"*Duane, I think the bulls went back into Greyhound.*"

"*Nope. They just ran through downtown Keystone and they're headed north.*"

I regrouped. The bulls had crossed through old Keystone and attracted more of the locals to join in the hunt. Two guys on four wheelers drove repeatedly up and down the logging road the bulls were on, which led north toward the Keystone Wye, reporting back to us their location. Of course, they kept pushing them north to the Keystone Wye, where only a barbed wire fence separated them from the four lane Highway 16.

In the evening light I finally caught sight of the first bull. Turning to my passenger with the high-powered rifle (I did not have one) I told him, "*You wanted to shoot a buffalo. Shoot that one.*" He responded by shoving the rifle into my hands. He said he had four bullets. When I sighted through his scope, all I could see was hair. I tried to trace out where the bull's ear was, fired, staggered the bull, but did not drop him. I shot again – same result. I told him I could not see through his scope. He said, "Dial it back." I shot again and killed the bull. One bullet left and one bull to go. I was getting nervous. The second bull stepped into a small clearing, and with the one remaining bullet, I shot him in the ear and killed him. I handed the man back his gun.

I asked Duane if he had any knives.

"No."

"A saw?"

"No."

I field dressed the two bulls with my three-inch folding knife and was bloody to my shoulders. We called our friend Bob Butterfield from the Hill City Standard Station to come with his homemade wrecker and we loaded the bulls in my pickup. We again imposed on Art Richardson. It made for a late night.

It was never our first option to kill escaped bulls, and we had many successes in shagging them back to the park. But we didn't hesitate to pull the trigger when public safety was at stake.

Roundup threats

The annual fall roundup had become a major tourism event, and as such, drew nationwide attention. Not everyone who became interested in the roundup was a friend or a fan. I began getting threatening mail about the roundup in the summer of 2001. An unnamed environmentalist group said they were going to disrupt the roundup and cut our fences to protest our annual bison herd handling activities. There were three such threats that came by mail that summer, which I passed on to the park superintendent, and he in turn passed them up the chain of command. Soon there were meetings, and more meetings, and more meetings, with agencies like SD Highway Patrol, Custer County Sherriff's Office, SD Department of Criminal Investigation, Division of Wildlife law enforcement. When the day of the roundup finally came, our hay yard at the corrals became their operations center; the South Visitor Center became the designated protest site. The amassed law enforcement muscle was impressive. The roundup came and went, but nothing happened except elevated stress levels.

A new kind of hunt

I constantly looked for opportunities to maximize revenues from the park's bison herd. All these revenues went into the park's revolving fund which financed the entire operation. We tried to develop an upgraded, high priced buffalo bull hunt on horseback based out of a back-country camp. We hired an outfitter to provide the camp, the meals, and the horses. Our camp was in the middle of the French Creek Canyon.

We tried to market the hunt through various hunting magazines, and that's where we drew the attention from People for the Ethical Treatment of Animals. The emails started coming, some signed; most were anonymous. Some were long epistles about the evils of hunting, but the one I remember was short and to the point: *"I hope you fall down and shoot yourself!"* We were only able to sell one hunt and discontinued it after two years. Not every venture was successful.

Dealing with drought

Dry cycles come to the park in roughly ten-year intervals. In general, the even numbered decades tended to be dryer than normal, the odd numbered decades tended to be wetter than normal. Dry cycles were simply part of the patterns to be managed.

We adjusted the stocking levels of both the bison and the elk herds in the fall with live buffalo sales and hunting seasons, in order to set up the grazing demand for the following summer. The big guess was "How much grass will we grow next summer?" and that estimate came in two parts. Those parts were addressed by 1) Updating our range condition map and 2) Estimating next year's precipitation.

We periodically updated our range condition map. Native prairie is a mixture of grasses, a different mix for different range sites. There are seven range types that make up the 21,000 acres of rangeland in the park. Each type has one of four condition classes (excellent, good, fair, poor) assigned depending on the grass species mix, and each condition had a unique production rate.

For example, a stony hills range site in excellent condition produces .9 Animal Unit Months (AUM's) of grazing per acre per year. The same range site in good condition produces .7 AUM's per acre per year. Field surveys determine condition. The closer the actual species mix was to the climax mix (the optimum native grass mix the site was capable of hosting), the better the condition. These updated surveys provided an answer to the first part of question, "How much grass will we grow next summer?" The actual range condition for the seven range types gives us the production figures for a normal year of precipitation.

33

The second part of the problem was estimating what percentage of normal precipitation we could realistically expect. Our theory was that the upcoming year's precipitation would consist of 80% of the current year's and 20% of the previous year's precipitation, a weighted two-year moving mean. When applied to the updated production estimates, we got our estimate. For example, if the past year's precipitation total was 15 inches, and the year's previous was 14 inches, the calculation would be: $[(.8X15) + (.2X14)]/16.5=90\%$ of normal production estimates. The normal precipitation for CSP rangelands is 16.5 inches.

The method worked very well. We annually made our fall adjustments to herd numbers to match predicted grazable forage amounts based on range conditions and precipitation expectations.

Drought exerts an emotional toll, but the emotional toll can be handled; we did that with reasonable success. Over the decades we experienced up-trending range conditions over the 21,000 acres of native grassland in the park. Coupled with other management efforts such as prescribe burning, we even accelerated range improvement. This tends to buffer the toll of drought.

Drought can bring about the baser levels of human nature. In the 80s we had to deal with chronic levels of cattle trespass. One neighboring rancher admitted to me that he watched some of his cows work a hole in the park fence to get to better grass. Capturing the trespass cattle was just part of the realities of drought. The local brand inspector helped us identify their owner; we always returned trespass cattle without penalty.

Chapter 2. The Work of Fire

The southern Black Hills are a fire-dependent environment. The vegetation types that thrive there depend on fire to renew them and beat back the less desirable invasive species. Fire cleanses the environment and reduces fuel loading (accumulated burnable materials) to acceptable levels. If the southern hills environments are subjected to fire on a regular basis, fire ceases to be a destructive force and becomes a friend. Applying fire to the landscape in a constructive way and dealing with the destructive force of unplanned wildfire is a constant challenge for the park and those responsible for such work. Dick Sparks was my fire forester for many years. He and I both knew that things can and do go awry, however the importance of the work requires that it go forward. The reality is that we need fire to maintain a healthy environment.

> You burn and are burned
> Yet the work must go forward.
> You sear and are seared
> By the flames bright and lively.
> Great accountability.

The local office of the National Weather Service (NWS) was available to us for spot weather forecasts. We used them routinely for wildfire suppression. We had to provide them with wet/dry bulb thermometer readings and with ground level wind speed and direction. In the case of prescribed burns, we had set up an actual weather station with recording devices to document weather patterns. In later years, the NWS had personnel on site for spot forecasts for prescribed burns.

We did a prescribed burn on the east side of the Wildlife Loop Road, an 1100-acre block, in the spring of 2001. Preparations for the burn took place over seven years, beginning with a timber sale specially designed to manage the fuel load for the upcoming burn. The perimeter required whole tree harvesting which left us big slash piles to dispose of. We burned the piles during the winter months after the purchaser completed the timber harvest. We had specially designed elk cover areas which were left as thicker stands of trees. Those areas were to be ignited early in the burn to limit the heat on them.

The day of the burn finally came. We did a test burn on the north end of the unit because the NWS predicted a southerly flow for the day, although the initial flow was northerly. "It's changing as we speak!" was their assurance. When you ring-fire a unit (igniting the unit along its perimeter), it is best to work into the wind so the head fire doesn't bump and challenge your control lines. It also keeps the smoke from obscuring the unit so if you have areas to pre-ignite, you can see to work.

We checked with the NWS again on the seemingly persistent northerly flow. "It's changing as we speak;" so we decided to begin firing from the north end of the unit to ignite the perimeter of the burn. I was conducting the interior ignition from a helicopter. We got halfway around the unit, and the wind continued stubbornly from the north. I had to overrule the NWS, and pulled the firing crews, moving them to the south end, and began firing into the wind. The NWS stopped answering the radio; I was told later they had left. The helicopter pilot refused to continue with the interior ignition because smoke covered the unit.

As I spent a last few minutes over the burn, my own emotions vacillated between fear, disappointment and determination not to lose the burn. I wanted to try to pre-ignite another elk cover area, but the pilot just shook his head; too smoky, too dangerous. A tremendous fire whorl pierced the smoke now covering the unit. It was elk cover area number two.

We managed to hang on to the perimeter of the burn, although much planning and years of preparation were badly altered because of a missed wind direction in a weather forecast. The burn was much hotter than we would have preferred. As a result, we lost all of our elk cover areas.

This is the world of prescribe burning. In spite of our best efforts of planning and preparation, things go awry. In this case it was a wind direction in a weather forecast. The work of fire will humble you, but it can make you rejoice. It will thrill you, but it can scare you. It will bring renewal, but it can bring destruction. It will bless you, but it can also bite you.

Ode to the Prairie Fire

Across the wide grassland
There's coming a fire.
We lit it with purpose
So all could admire
The grass that would thrive
Though some would expire.

'Cross upland and lowland
A quick smoky spire,
A flash fiery furnace.
All natives aspire
To survive it alive;
It's what they require.

Searing encroachment,
Pines hate the wildfire.
Bluegrass is speechless,
Cheat grasses expire
While bluestems revive
With a green needle choir.

Prairie fires give opportunity
Where natives and invaders strive
Restoring grassland community
Only the best will survive.

April Fool's Day 1981

The fire was quiet now, on the ground.
My hand crew was nowhere to be found.
It was smoky and I was so very thirsty.
Across the road the slope was black;
Two fire trucks silent, on the tarmac
But everyone was gone.
At the "Ball Diamond" I could see the blaze
Down in the canyon, a fiery haze
Embers raining, dozens of little fires.
"Maybe the Texas Snow Job will save the day;
We'll soon see if it's good as they say."
Crews made their stand on the Ghost Canyon Road.

A tent, sleepless night
Awful roaring rumbling sounds
Tree tops like freight trains
My insides were turning 'round
Listening to the awful sounds

A group of friends all took their turn
They prayed for me; it was my burn.

Fire and Smoke

    Western forests need their fire
    Fuel loads will surely burn.
    Nature's way will oft' require
    Wood to ash a swift return.
    The fire is born by lightning flash;
    Needles explode into flame.
    It's nature's way to take out trash
    So forest health can be reclaimed.
    When the forest fills with fuel,
    The consequence of forest life,
    Fire is the natural tool
    And flame is like the surgeon's knife.
    So know the system isn't broke
    When western skies are filled with smoke.

Coming home, July 6, 1988

1988 was a nine-inch rainfall year for the park, capping off a decade of drought. It was the same year Yellowstone burned.

I was on vacation when Ken called.

"It's 10,000 acres now."

"What are you talking about?"

"The park's on fire."

A rented plane, a long flight back to Custer; we picked up the heavy smoke drift at Pierre. When we reached the park, there were five smoke columns like towering grain silos rising from the north rim of French Creek; we had to detour around them. At Custer, only the mountain tops poked through the smothering quilt of smoke.

"We can't land here; going back to the park," said the pilot

The park airspace was closed. Aircraft incoming, outgoing, 2 o'clock, 5 o'clock, 10 o'clock, 1 o'clock.

"When we touch down, you jump out right away. I'm tossing your bag on the tarmac, and I'm outta' here."

Blackie, the air traffic control boss for the fire, was running at us, waving and shouting; he was not a welcoming committee. When he saw it was me, he went back to the hanger. I was home, but home was on fire.

When Fire Comes to Visit

Oh visit us often, consuming fire
and burn away the clutter dire
of sticks and needles, cones and wood
that choke and shade and kill, and could
if left undone, destroy the forest all;
when flame comes to visit and fire comes to call.

It's not the fire a villain to fear
but the clutter that's stacked in year by year
that threatens life itself, to be sent
back to its basic element.
It instantly explodes when purifying fire
comes to call and clean, ask and inquire.

Oh flame, examine all that's hid
and burn to ash the trash, and rid
us of the gathering load
of encumbrances that silently bode
us to smother and choke and die.
The flame bids us go where freedoms lie.

So come to me often, Spirit of fire.
Burn away the dross, and inquire
of my clutter, the waste within,
and free me from the peril of my sin
so the grandness of all that's free
can bloom and grow and flower in me.

The work is weighty
It's not for the faint hearted.
Each and every time
Your career is on the line;
Each and every fiery time.

I have long admired the managers at Wind Cave National Park for the job they have done in managing the rangelands of Wind Cave with prescribed burning. They have kept at it year by year, been aggressive with it, and have persevered through the inevitable flaws inherent in the practice. They viewed escapes (burned acres outside the original control lines) as bonus acres burned. We worked with them on several occasions.

In 2003, CSP and WCNP did a cooperative burn on our south boundary, their north, which was the largest burn to date in the Black Hills, nearly 4,000 acres. CSP's need for prescribed burning is great, but more complex than our neighbor to the south, due to the fact that CSP is two-thirds forestland. Higher fuel loadings and tighter controls for flame height and duration are needed. Forest burns are more expensive, and to take advantage of the economies of scale (larger burns cost less per acre than smaller burns) we need to do larger forest burns, yet the need for controls do not decrease. The path of least resistance is to back off and do nothing, yet the responsible thing to do is to press ahead. It takes fortitude and courage, confidence and resilience because it is inevitable that at some point, things will not go according to plan in spite of the best preparation and execution. I hope political critics recognize the necessity of the use of fire and treat practitioners with an appropriate mercy.

Chapter 3. The Human Story

Discovering the human story of the park is both fascinating and necessary. We desire to know who came before us; it's in our corporate DNA.

We explored a cave shelter reported to me by an anonymous tourist on the south end of the Wildlife Loop Road with the help of the Office of the State Archeologist. Dr. Fred Sellet and Mike Fosha worked during the summers of 2000 and 2001, digging two adjacent one-meter square exploration pits that surveyed the soil horizons in that shelter to a depth of four meters. They piece-plotted every cultural artifact, and in the process, surveyed 2500 years of continuous human habitation.

The living floors in the shelter are separated with thin, non-cultural bearing sand strata, likely the result of periodic inundations of valley flood waters. Fred, Mike and the volunteer crew from the State Archeologist's office found stone tools, cooking fire pits, stone heating pots, bone fragments, a dog's stone coffin- all encountered in the square meter snapshots of the page-like living floors.

I initiated the exploration by promoting the site to Mike Fosha. I wanted to assist in the excavation, but I got fired from that task; I didn't demonstrate enough care with the artifacts. "You're too crude," was Mike's assessment of my skills. I still observed the fascinating treasure hunt when time allowed. When the National Science Foundation grant ran out to do the exploration, I had the walls sheeted and the top closed. Sadly, it has remained that way since 2001. Somewhere among those strata is the living floor reflecting a giant leap of technology on the Great Plains, the transition from atlatl throwing to bow and arrow shooting; a transition that rivals the significance of the internet in today's generation. The place oozes with story, just waiting to be discovered and told. There is still at least one meter, and maybe several more, to explore until we reach the bedrock floor of the cave. Will the earliest living floors reveal the lives of the hill's earliest inhabitants, the Clovis, Folsom, and Plano people? We want to know and we need to know their story, because in a sense, it's our story too. Journey with me in the next three poems into the world of those who have gone before.

Movie Draw

    They came and stayed in times long past,
    the hunters came while in their prime.
    Their evidences were off cast
    and hidden in a downward climb,
    layered in an earthy grime.
    They lived and tried to carve a life
    out of an ancient paradigm,
    those makers of the stone blade knife.

The valley was a glad contrast
to dry and dusty desert clime.
Here the bones of rich repasts
were cast from many dinnertimes.
How many lived this ancient rhyme
and found escape from droughty strife
to eat their creek-side suppertime;
the makers of the stone blade knife?

The Avon Lea returns would last
three thousand seasons of springtime.
The generations came and passed
to spend their sunny wintertime;
flakes from fireside stone pastime,
labors of a stone-age wife,
a thousand children's pantomime,
these makers of the stone blade knife.

Traces of a past lifetime
are hidden in the sands of time.
They rest now in the afterlife,
the makers of the stone blade knife.

A story revealed in
Current stony quietness
The past violence
A hunter's grim evidence
In forestland loneliness

Stone Blind

The old stone hunting blind
Stands ever quiet, solitary.
The elk pass by, they even tarry
Though for killing t'was designed.
The hunter crouches low, confined
Behind rocks looking ordinary;
Peers at the elk, ever wary
But soon to feed this human kind.
And with a quick decisive throw,
Aiming fast his deadly dart,
He lets his levered spear tip go
Straight to his quarry's beating heart;
He emerges with his stony knife.
It's what he knew, his way of life.

I've seen two of these stone blinds during my time in the park. It appears these blinds were made for small men. They are mid-thigh in height, discounting sedimentation, and about three feet in diameter. Both blinds are in a currently forested environment and made of loosely stacked native stone. The hunter would crouch down inside that circular wall of stone, waiting for their quarry to move close enough for a kill with an atlatl or in later times, with bow and arrow. These early hunters had to be patient. Their people depended upon their hunting skills for their survival.

The Roof in Movie Draw

There was a time when the roof was grand,
the roof that covered the floor of sand
at the cave in Movie Draw, where a
hundred generations of my people came to camp
and hunt and live.

The roof was sandstone rock, as firm and
resolute as a roof could be, and always would be.
It sheltered my grandfathers and it shelters me.
It's been there as long as anyone's memory
could recall.

Today the solid old roof lies broken on the ground.
The life we knew could never pass is found to be no more
The stones lay scattered in their own
graveyard in the grass. My stone roof is gone.

When my father died, his shelter, always there for me
broke off. When he became no more than a memory
a piece of my security lay broken on the grass.
The solid old roof opened
to the sky.

There was a time when the cave was deep and cool
and shady, and we could fashion a stone tool
in comfort on the hottest summer day, or take
a nap or softly play as we lazily whiled our
time away.

But imperceptibly over time the floor rose.
My growth accelerated in the old stone cave,
and the roof lowered to meet my rising hand,
while the growing numbers in our band made
their impact on the land.

The storms brought layers of silt and sand
that covered the record of our band.
A clean floor, but a covered memory
of life as it was, but is no more.
I cannot go back.

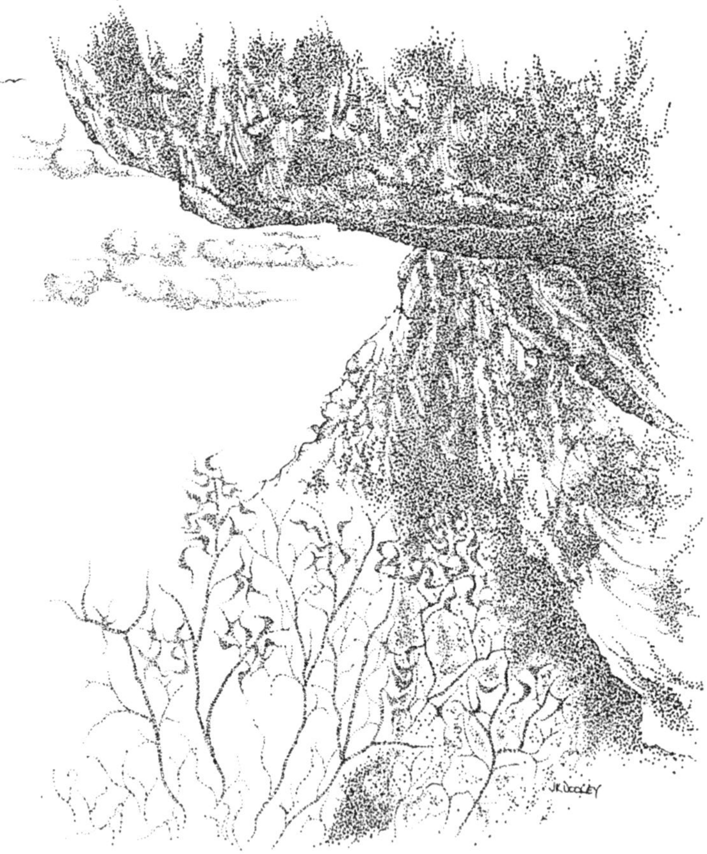
JK DOOLEY

Chapter 4. Horses

Horses have long been part of the cultural fabric of the park; their use in resource management has been relatively recent. Dodger, a two-year-old gelding purchased in 1995, became the first CSP- owned saddle horse. Several more followed as the use of horses became part of the resource management tool chest, especially in bison management. Through horses, we could become "one with them," even though we cannot be "one of them." They gave us a four-footed presence among four-footed creatures allowing us a speed and mobility equal to our counterparts. My steady riding horse, Red, was a ten-year-old ranch gelding purchased in 1996.

A True Buffalo Horse

When Red first came, I'd overcome
his quirks and demons exorcise.
His temperament was troublesome,
but his speed, I'd come to realize,
was like a jet plane in disguise.
And although he was a little coarse,
it wasn't long till I'd surmise
Red was a true buffalo horse.

Over time he'd be my chum,
and on his back I'd supervise
a host of riders, venturesome
for buffalo herds at bright sunrise
on horses wet with exercise.
When bully cows obstruct the course
and cause for close work would arise,
Red was the true buffalo horse.

I wish for time's moratorium
where old joints would not agonize
to make steep travel burdensome.
Too late do we become cow wise.
Too soon the years do penalize.
Red's gone now, and I'm past remorse.
But over time I'll idolize
Red, a tried true buffalo horse.

Red could use his sixteen size
to meet the bully cows with force.
Those that knew him recognize
That Red was a true buffalo horse.

Horses, as tools of management, also had their intrinsic personalities. Sometimes they seemed to reflect the personalities of those around us.

Old Prideful

Prideful is a willful horse,
ears laid back, tail sucked in,
bit clenched hard, defying him.
He's on a domination course.
Prideful is a foolish horse
doing silly things to win;
no time wrong for battle grim,
he often chooses brutal force.
Prideful's a deceptive horse
with a self-congratulating grin.
Thoughts of self exclude remorse,
thinks life is all about just him.
Prideful's not like me of course.
Prideful's only just a horse.

The Bad Spoiled Filly

A difficult horse – a bad spoiled filly
Resistive of all authority
Full of surprises – a daffy down dilly,
To have her own way's the priority
'Cause obedience shows inferiority!
The cowboy can ride but the filly won't learn
She struggles for superiority.
Defiance persists, rebelliousness burns
Her attitude hardens – a difficult turn.
She's green broke trained, but really untamed
A joyless mount, a cause for concern
'Cause sooner or later the cowboy gets maimed.
Her submission could make such a beautiful pair
But this stubborn filly's at best a brood mare.

Four-legged brother
Makes us one with otherness
See life differently
Move with horse impunity
In another community.

Swimming in the River

    Five hundred head down the Lame Johnny fence
    A cold snowy day; all trucks except Cliff and me.
    Nearly there, a quarter mile from the trap gate
    When, by our own negligence
    An unfixed hole in the division fence
    And cows flowed through the gaping breach
    Like a river – fifty head in a flood.
    Cliff and I waded into the flow,
    Swept through by a current of buffalo,
    Spilling out the other side.
    We were one with them in that swift ride

One in a flowing brown wooly tide
Until we could ride ahead of the flood
And turn the river back again.

Horses enable
A remarkable moment
One with otherness
In a river of bison
Running, floating with the elk.

Running with the elk

A long ride in the early spring;
Chad, Richard, and I took a morning to put 15 miles on horses,
North Farm to the corrals.
As we neared the corrals and climbed to the Racetrack saltlick,
There before us was a herd of elk, taking minerals.
Two of the horses were "dragging their toes" tired
But Red still had energy, and on quick impulse
We ran into the center of the elk.
As they departed, we left with them.
Running and grunting, shifting right and left in unison,
The elk completely surrounded Red and me
As he ran and floated along with them.
I gave Red his head, and for an amazing quarter mile
We were one with them.

We skidded to a stop at the southern escarpment, and the elk herd split in two, half turning east and the other half turning west.
It's not often you can ride as one with the elk. Horses added to the adventure, giving access to events that lodge in your mind and heart. I look back on them with fondness in that crazy world of "horseback."

Exhilaration
Riding fast in hot pursuit
Hoof beat on hoof beat
Muscle rippling in the wind
Mane and tail running freely

When it came time to handle our sale stock, we'd have to gather them from the 'kill pasture,' a 300-acre unit north of the corrals. While other workers drove four- wheel drive pickups, my preference was to ride Red. He exuded some kind of dominance with buffalo. Even though there were times when he had cow horns tangled in his tail, he was never marked.

The gather from the kill pasture was a fast-paced affair; the 350 or so head of buffalo moved swiftly across the prairie. Red and I pounded along amongst the pickups, but when they had to stop for steep draws or water ways, Red and I catapulted over the edges and cross the draws with agility and speed. Each time we made a kill pasture run, I would remark to myself, "What a rush!" as I stroked Red's long auburn neck.

> **Nasty charging cows**
> **Big horse speaking bad cow talk**
> **Spurring, hard charging**
> **One of us must turn aside.**
> **Red dominates, overcomes.**

Red's Last Great Ride

Red's last great ride came on the heels of Buddy's catastrophe. I hauled Buddy home from the vet to the North Farm to recuperate from his gore wound earlier that morning. Returning to the corrals, I saw the morning's crew on Race Track Butte. They were at a standoff with cows that refused another step south.

Red was the only horse left at the corrals, so Red it was. We slowly climbed the slopes to the butte, every step an exercise of pain for Red's arthritic shoulders and hips. Finally, reaching the top, we saw the twenty riders standing in small clusters about a hundred yards from the herd; the buffalo massed along the south side of the butte, and our destination, the trap gate in plain view a half mile away. A single blue pickup was trying to dislodge the herd from the butte, but to no avail. There were a dozen cows scattered throughout the herd that gave chase to any rider that dared to venture too close. It truly was a standoff. So was to begin Red's final great ride.

We had climbed the east side of the butte, so we worked from east to west, teasing the first bully cow from the bunch. Out she came, head down blowing snot, coming straight for us. Red seemed to transform at that instant from an arthritic 20-year-old to a warhorse. I wheeled him toward the cow and spurred, charging the charging cow; it was a game of high stakes chicken. With about 20 feet between us, the cow turned off. Cow number one. *"Way to go, Red!"*

We moved slowly toward the west, teased out the second cow. She charged, we charged. Cow number two. Red had gotten his blood up; no stopping now. Cow number three, four, five, halfway across the herd. When we got to the west end and had faced down about a dozen, the herd was ready to move. I motioned to the other riders and we pushed the herd off the butte through the gate into the park's south unit to await the roundup day.

Having closed the gate, we walked back to the corrals in a loose parade of horses and riders. No one pulled along-side us, but I could hear some of the chatter. *"I didn't know you could do that."* In my mind, I responded, *"You can't. Don't try it."* But Red was special; he made some kind of mysterious, dominating communication to those belligerent cows. I unsaddled him at the hitching post, and as I brushed him down, I told him, *"You the man Red. You the man!"*

Horses also had their useful life. It was a sad day when the chapter turned for one of these beloved co-workers, and Red was no exception.

Selling Red

I decided I must sell him – he was twenty.
His joints pained him, especially on the hills
And he needed an easier life
Than what the park demanded of him.
It was auction day; we'd run up the calves
Then Red was put on display
There at the hitching post.
The time came to ride him into the sale ring.
Forward, back, right, left, crack my whip.
I told the crowd about him
And that I dreaded this day
But he needed an easier life.
I stepped off, pulled saddle and hackamore
And he went away to the highest bidder.
Goodbye Red, goodbye old friend. It's time to retire.

Chasing, being chased
Turnabout is fair enough
Take care with the bulls
They will dominate a horse
And strike you if they can.

Getting Chased

Each spring we'd clear all the buffalo from the south unit of the park – the R&D, an old name from the days of its acquisition. With the south unit cleared, we established a buffer between CSP bulls and Wind Cave National Park bulls, thereby preserving our fence during the inevitable combat of breeding season. The bulls often hung back after the cow herd exited and clearing them took extra time. We had to watch the gates leading to the north to which we could drive, and occasionally ride the timber, deep draws and mesas comprising the park's south unit. We thought the unit was clear, so I took the opportunity to catch an afternoon ride on Red one spring day, and take a final tour of the R&D.

I saw him in the timber; big, aged, solitary, winter fur hanging in strips from his shoulders, dust rolling off from his wallow, defying any interference with his sunny afternoon dust bath. When Red and I moved a little too close for his liking, he responded by... being a bull. The chase was on; the bull was the chaser and we were the hunted. Red and I pounded through the timber, the old bull in hot pursuit, the pace fast and getting faster.

"When is he going to give this up? Red, I hope you don't stumble."

We pounded along, a quarter, half, three-quarters of a mile, the bull 20 yards behind us. He was not giving up. I kept glancing over my shoulder as the trees flashed by in the afternoon sun. Finally, at about a mile, nearly at Teakettle Draw, the bull pulled up turning north. When we got a hundred yards between us, I eased Red off too, and we parted company with the old boy. He'd exit a day later through the Teakettle Gate. A pleasant ride on a spring day to give a last look at a supposedly vacated south unit, a hostile bull and a long chase with a fast-enough horse, all the makings of a memorable spring afternoon.

Dodger and the Iron Creek Bull

The bull in the timber was hazard fraught
As he lay in a thicket of dog hair pine.
Richard and Vern both stated their thought
That I should go in and disturb his recline.
It was Dodger and I – he was the equine.
We suspected the bull had an ornery streak;
He'd often trespassed the boundary line.
That bull had a liking for Iron Creek.

So Dodger pushed into the woody plot
To move him away from the boundary line.
My .22 pistol was full of snake shot;
To pepper him often was my design.
But one shot and Dodge was a bucking freak
When buffy jumped up expressing repine;
That bull had a liking for Iron Creek.

I'd cocked and readied a second shot
But Dodger's wild bucking would undermine
Sitting tight in the saddle as I ought.
My carcass went airborne in the sunshine
With Dodger acting so infantine,
And on the way down my pistol did speak.
The bull took off from the timberline,
That bull with a liking for Iron Creek.

Although my horse, Dodger, I could malign,
He stood close by so I could seek
To climb back on and chase hotline,
The bull with a liking for Iron Creek.

He's Back at Iron Creek

In spite of our best efforts, changing a bull's mind is not always successful. I suppose, like a lot of us, it takes adequate trauma to affect a permanent change of behavior. Such was the case for the Iron Creek bull. Later that spring, the park office again received complaints that a Custer State Park bull was frequenting the US Forest Service's Iron Creek Horse Camp.

The federal employees and horse campers at Iron Creek horse camp did not appreciate the high adventure of a cantankerous old bull in their campground. He would have given them such great things to talk about on their coffee breaks. But no..., they insisted that we move him away for the sake of boring tranquility.

Vern and I trailered Buddy and Red up to Iron Creek to try again. We would attempt to move him south at least one or two drainages and hoped to affect a more permanent change of behavior so he'd quit terrorizing those poor Forest Service employees and their campground guests. We found the bull in his favorite spot, square in the middle of the campground so he could easily keep his eye on everything and react with belligerence to each and every disturbance. Vern and I circled behind him to the north, salted him once with snake shot, and started him south at a brisk clip. He crossed the dilapidated old fence with two horses in hot pursuit. The open range law says, "If you want to keep cattle off your property, you are responsible to fence them out." Somehow this did not apply here.

The trail was, well, a trail, so the three of us were pounding along single file. Every time the bull even thought about turning on us to do battle, Vern popped him with another round of snake shot (#12 shot in a .22 caliber cartridge) in the behind. This went on for a quarter mile until Vern exhausted his ammunition, which was a concern because that bull really liked the Iron Creek Campground from which he was so rudely expelled, and I could tell he was not happy with the two that ejected him.

I yelled over the hoof beats that I had nine more shots on the ready, and "pull over so I could pass." Red and I pulled in behind the bull. I leveled my little snake shot shooter between Red's ears and proceeded to shift the Iron Creek bull into successively higher gears. Red never flinched, or at least if he did, we were moving far too fast for him to get balky about the whole thing. By the time the ninth round exited my barrel, we had reached Mach 1 and were flying past the second drainage.

Vern and I finally pulled up, and grinning to each other, watched the bull disappear over the ridge maintaining a ridiculously high rate of speed. I suppose he had stories to tell the other bulls when breeding season started a month later. He never came back to Iron Creek, where the Forest Service employees and campers could now return to their ordinary routines.

Chapter 5. Tapestry

A tapestry looks quite different, front and back. The front shows a pattern and picture that makes sense; it may even have a degree of beauty. The back side – not so much. As I conclude my park song with this final chapter, I offer some more of both sides of my tapestry. With some things I can see the makings of a pattern, with others the pattern is still taking shape. Let me encourage you to figure out your own tapestry. Pay attention to the events in your life. Are there patterns emerging? Keep a journal. Remember. Consider.

On Leadership

    The leadership road is a selfless trail
    Where others claim what the leader began.
    He charts the vision, helps them prevail
    Knowing they'll outshine the veteran.
    He enjoys the trust of the high placed man,
    Often to play interceder.
    Then becoming an obscure part of the plan;
    Thus the way of the one called leader.

    His willing ear listens to other's travail.
    He plays the part of the clergyman.
    His own complaint does he downscale;
    A strained heart disguised comedian.
    Many grasp acclaim, though charlatan,
    And time will reveal the impeder.
    He truthfully leads his follower clan,
    Thus the way of the one called leader.

    Self-actualization's a fairy tale.
    He takes his cue from the fisherman.
    Other's success he'll gladly unveil,
    Though regarded only a best man.
    When his people really don't think they can
    He'll be their biggest cheerleader.
    He's his clan's best salesman,
    Thus the way of the one called leader.

    Though he's had his day like a Minute Man,
    He wants them to be the succeeder.
    So he'll step aside like a gentleman,
    Thus the way of the one called leader.

An Honest Face

When love is tested by affliction
Impure hearts are bathed in light.
Trouble shows the contradiction,
Revealing what's the wrong and right.
Trials reveal love's hesitation
When the love's for self alone.
Trials show our limitation,
How narrow and how selfish prone.
The proof of life is in the action,
Staying through to persevere;
Keeping hold of self's reaction,
Holding fast to love's good cheer.
Trials give an honest face
To what's inside the hiding place.

When trust is tested by betrayal,
Reality of love shows plain,
Showing self in grand portrayal
To see if faith can stand the strain.
Humility is sorely tested
With a shunning to endure.
The inner self is manifested
As an accurate portraiture.
When one's tested with the prodding
And nothing runs along the plan,
Yet when graciousness comes nodding
It shows the depth that's in the man.
Trials give an honest face
To what's inside the hiding place.

When hope is tested by the crushing
Of desire so deeply held;
Comes the news, a hot wind rushing

Through your chest, and hope is quelled.
Disappointments hard rough edge
Shakes your vision down its length
Blighted hopes can drive a wedge
Between your spirit and its strength.
Trials search out hope's real source
When desire is brushed aside;
When power pushes past remorse
And walks ahead though light has died.
Trials give an honest face
To what's inside the hiding place.

Our Lives at the North Farm

Our children grew up in the park. Their formative years were spent at the North Farm, the only remaining farmstead left in the park, and the only park residence on the Iron Mountain Road.

The old homestead was on the north boundary of the park. The story and a half log house had Appalachian style corners and was hewn flat inside with finished walls. It had four small bedrooms upstairs, and a bathroom, living room and kitchen/dining room down. The barn was of similar construction with a big loft. The garage was also log. Spokane Creek flowed past the place into a two-acre impoundment, and then made its way down Spokane Canyon.

We home schooled our three children, the oldest through sixth grade, the other two through eighth grade. It was a wonderful place for them to grow up. They learned to play. We had very poor television reception, but the park's two-way radio sat on a shelf in the kitchen. I think it provided ample entertainment for young minds.

We lived there for fourteen years. Our private lives and my work life were truly blended during those years, and in many ways are the back side of the tapestry. Sandy was our family's golden retriever and is a small snapshot of our family's experience during those years.

Sandy

    Sandy came when the kids were small,
    The runt of a puppy litter.
    Her gentle jaws a carry all,
    She the faithful baby sitter.
    She brought home neighbor's shoes and bowls,
    A gold retriever trait;
    Sixteen years of home patrols
    And waiting at the gate.
    Her ears went deaf and eyes went dim,
    Her white face ghostly older.
    Life for her became so grim,
    Red tumor on her shoulder.
    She climbed the ridge line by my side
    And sadly, by my hand, she died.

Each morning I drove the Iron Mountain Road to the office. During the summer season there would be lots of traffic, but in the late fall, winter, and spring, the road was an extension of our driveway, and during those times, we noticed every vehicle that came up the road. It was just part of home for my family.

The Iron Mountain Road

> I'd drive the Iron Mountain Road
> a couple times a day.
> The morning trip was mine to pray,
> a thankful episode
> that Custer Park was my abode,
> and the winter road my way.
> I loved to see this brand new day!
> Fulfilling work to me did bode.
> Such was my pleasure at morning's dawn,
> an elk herd, an old bison bull,
> a donkey jam, a doe and fawn.
> With sunrise gold light visible,
> Seeing a massive prairie lawn,
> I'm graced by all that's beautiful.

Indian Summer

When the oak trees turn to brown
and the ashes turn to gold,
the buffalo hair's like wooly down
to face the winter cold,
yet the Indian summer lingers
before hard and icy sleet;
bare arms and open fingers
soak in the sunny heat.
Bull elk squeal in dim lit dawn
for cow elk negligee,
and fall rains green the prairie lawn
that o'er summer withered grey.
Enjoy the Indian summer days
and learn her gentle golden ways.

Office time

It was my intent to get away from the office and the desk half the time, a goal that was often assaulted by the tyranny of the urgent. Budgets, reports, personnel, meetings, planning, administrative demands, all these were necessary parts of leading the Resource Management team, yet they also insulated me from the heart beat of the park. I made an effort to remain connected in tangible ways to this special place and the life that pulsed through its veins.

Roped, harnessed, and hobbled

Time gets too short for riding
And schedules too cropped for horses.
I'm roped by impatient forces
And goaded by endless insiding.
My trail cuts deep with the sliding
Down worn out well traveled courses.
I'm harnessed by endless discourses
And hobbled where duty's residing.
How I'd go to where freedom's presiding,
Far from duty and imposed remorses
That pull down my head with the chiding
Of laws that the do list enforces.
How I'd go with liberty stridin'
And crash on just ridin' and slidin'

I satisfied my need to "go ridin' and slidin'" by getting out, by being part of prescribe burns (I loved running the firing operations), by administering an occasional timber sale, by helping move buffalo when needed. These were some of the things that got me out so that I, too, could enjoy the natural rhythms of the park. I often told my crew, "If it's not any fun, what's the point?" I learned to enjoy those rhythms and match their pace as much as I could. "There is a time for all things under heaven..." Much of the rhythm was set by the animals and their seasons. There were times to go fast and times that afforded the opportunity to slow down and enjoy the park. I learned that it was foolish not to observe their pace.

Meadowlark's After all

When a pause in the admin tune
Meant I could escape for an hour
On a balmy April afternoon,
I'd go to the corrals in the park
To hear the happy language
Of a returning Meadowlark.

Sitting in sunshine on posts piled high
With breezes blowing welcome warmth
And Sandhill voices in the sky,
Yet the sweetest sound of anything
Were the welcome cry of Meadowlarks
Returning in the spring.

It was therapy to my soul,
A sign that things were right
And that my life was whole;
And that all the administrative gall
Was not the last word
After all, after all, after all.

The politics of fencing and Pierre

The complex behind Legion Lake Lodge began as the Nils A. Boe Youth Forestry Camp. It was awarded to the Department of Corrections (DOC) as a place for a juvenile detention center, with an emphasis on establishing a mutually beneficial arrangement for the park. There was Camp One and Camp Two; both camps provided work crews for the park. Camp One put out three timber crews and Camp Two put out two maintenance crews. The crews put in an eight-hour day and were schooled in work skills and work ethic during their adjudicated time there.

The timber crews began by doing much needed thinning work in the park's forestland. Their work expanded to include occasional trail construction, but their mainstay became fencing. The timber crews became formidable fencing crews under the leadership of Roger Breske, the park's liaison to those crews. They removed and replaced many miles of perimeter and interior fence. All of the interior fence and about two-thirds of the perimeter fence were the product of their labors. We produced our own wooden posts. I would make sure our timber sales included some POL (products other than logs- trees between 6 and 8 inches in diameter) and then buy the POL decks from the sale purchasers at the end of their contracts.

Camp #1 crews would process the POL decks into posts, peel them with our processer, and we would haul them to Rapid City to have them treated. Those posts went into park fencing. The Resource Program also made investments into explosives and all that went with them; air hose, pneumatic hammers, rock bits, a powder magazine, detonation cord and caps, a portable air compressor.

We began to use high tensile woven wire to reduce the repair need caused by moving elk herds. The four-foot wire panels reportedly have total rebound when pushed to the ground. The young men of Camp #1 took pride in the excellent fences resulting from their labors, and the benefit to the park was enormous.

For many years CSP enjoyed a truly symbiotic relationship with Department of Corrections (DOC). Sadly, those days came to an end. The cause? I can only give my perspective. I think the Department of Corrections shifted to the paradigm that required these boys to be students in a classroom. Any other approach to their rehabilitation was unacceptable, including working and sweating, dealing with blisters, and taking pride in a job well done. This was a type of corrections too far outside the box for adjudicated young men. I think that was the problem.

Camp #1 and Camp #2 were moved south of Custer, and what was once a highly productive juvenile institution for young men became a girl's camp. The young men went to "Boot Camp," later called "Star Academy" which closed several years ago. Progress? Not for the park. Are adjudicated young men any better off? I don't know. Disciplined work on a fencing crew seemed to help a lot of young men get their bearings and gain a work ethic.

Fencing and neighbors

Replacing our west perimeter fence did not draw a positive response from some of the public. Although it relieved a lot of pressure on me by not having to chase escaped bulls much of the summer, it disrupted the activities of other people. Some hunters counted on having their favorite holes open so they could shoot elk or deer moving in or out of the park. One Sunday morning I received a phone call informing me that we had bulls out on the McClanahan Ranch on the west side of the park. The rest of our family went to church and I went to investigate.

Sure enough, there were seven bulls outside a newly replaced section of double panel woven wire fence. The YFC timber crews had just installed it earlier that summer. I was alone, and could not physically chase the bulls, only worry them, so I got their attention and slowly drove back and forth about 100 yards away. Thankfully, they retreated through the hole in the fence from which they had exited. I drove up to that spot to find our brand-new double panel fence cut from top to bottom. I spent the rest of the morning stretching and crimping both panels, wire by wire to knit the hole back together. I started a rumor by telling one of the members of the Custer bar crowd that if we ever caught someone cutting our fences, I would barb wire him to a tree and come back a couple days later to see if he was thirsty. The fence cutting stopped.

Christmas Trees and Pierre

In the early 1980's one of the "other duties as assigned" was to secure Christmas trees for the offices in the state capitol building, and of course, there was no office that turned down the prospect of a free Christmas tree from the park. The order was usually for thirty trees, which made "Christmas trees for Pierre" a week-long project.

One year I had scheduled my Christmas tree week, only to have the Deputy Secretary of Game Fish and Parks call and say the truck will be there Friday. This was on a Wednesday prior to my scheduled week, giving me one day. I had a Youth Forestry Camp (YFC) crew clearing a roadway for the new Sylvan Lake campground, an area with a lot of spruce in it, so I told the crew leader I needed to load 30 trees on a truck that Friday, and in my frustration said I didn't need to see them.

The next Tuesday the Park Superintendent got a call from the Department Secretary; "What is this, some kind of a joke?" I ended up in Pierre that December and thought, "How bad can those trees be?" I found one in the State Forestry District Office. The spacing between the branches was about 18 inches. They had hung a ball on the end of a branch and it drooped to the floor. They were truly 'Charlie Brown' trees, but nobody saw any humor whatsoever in them, except me. Nearly getting fired over Christmas trees did wonders for my Christmas spirit that year.

Prisoners and the forest

Forest management is vital, but 'quiet' work in the sense that it's seldom showy, often poorly understood by others, but mess it up and you will indeed attract attention. Keeping forests from stagnating due to overly dense conditions, structuring project work to enable some consistency in product output, limiting or mitigating the damages by disease, wildfire and weather, and using timber sales to accomplish a multiple of objectives kept the work challenging. One long term effort involved using trustee labor to treat the woodland devastation of a large snowstorm.

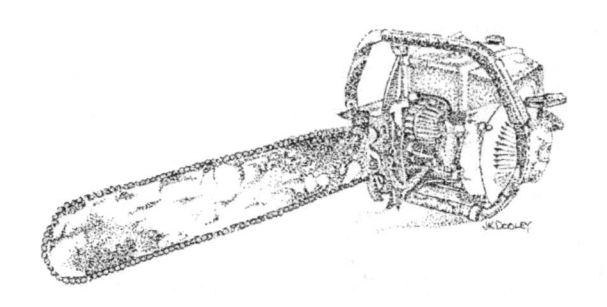

Forty Saws to the Woods

The storm descended with an uncommon fury. It began on April 20, 2000, and left three feet of heavy saturated snow, so full of water that a cross-section revealed a luminous blue tint. An occasional explosion came from the forest, the rifle shot of a breaking treetop, forever giving way to the strain. When the Iron Mountain Road was finally opened, I saw trees lying everywhere, broken, tipped out, or permanently bent over. I knew this would be bad.

I saw this kind of destruction before, setting up a timber sale in the Galena 4 timber unit, before the Galena Fire swept it all away. It was 20-25 acres of bent over pines, impenetrable; I got across it by stepping on the horizontal tree trunks three feet off the ground, thinking that if I ever fell, I'd never get out. It presented the worst fuel hazard I could imagine. This snowstorm would create a similar kind of damage.

As the days wore on, we began to assess the extent of the harm done. What we had on the roadsides, which we were working on with chippers and newly arrived inmates, was only the beginning of a big problem. We discovered four square miles of this kind of snow damage. Trustee labor was available to us, not free but mostly reasonable. We opened up our seasonal dorms for housing, purchased a fleet of chainsaws to supplement our own so as to enable forty men to begin the enormous task of 'brushing down' all that damage. That involved cutting up that sea of bent and broken trees so that the resultant fuels would lie close to the ground and thus decompose after a few years. We also piled fuels along strategically selected timber roads to establish fuel breaks, places where we could start a back burn if we ever had to deal with a wildfire in that mess.

Thus began a two-year project; hiring crew leaders, repairing saws, finding and mapping damaged areas, meeting with Department of Corrections officials, dealing with behavior issues, keeping books on the endless expenses, dealing with occasional injuries, and fighting constant attempts to divert that workforce to unrelated projects. We sent forty men to the woods every day, five and sometimes six days a week for two years. We logged a quarter million work hours dedicated to mitigating the havoc resulting from that one snowstorm.

After two years, the forest fell quiet again. Visitors had no idea of the effort expended. Timber management would go on and the deadly stagnation of forest stands in the park would gradually be corrected. Other catastrophes would generate big efforts, like timber salvage following large wildfires or battling a

Mountain Pine Beetle epidemic; but nothing in my experience would match the human drama of dealing with all that snow damaged timber.

Futility

>Standing in the forest trees
>Seeking the tranquility,
>Musing possibility
>Of balanced nature ease.
>There's the devil to appease
>In the system's volatility.
>Life loses viability
>Subjected to disease,
>Hoping cycles are of life
>Knowing spirals are of death.
>Within the beauty there is strife;
>The end of all is loss of breath.
>Environmental incivility
>Comes from natural futility.

Trails

Trails in the park were not always part of the Resource Management program. Visitor Services and Maintenance periodically put up a sign or made a map, but a lot of our trails just happened. A trail became established where people walked or liked to ride, and once established, a trail. The park ended up with a lot of haphazard trail development. In about 2000, I was asked to oversee the work of some summer volunteers who came with horses to "do trail work." A.J. and Helen Walters came from Michigan every summer for many years to work on trails. We started out by marking out an official trail system with blue plastic diamonds nailed to trees along trails we would maintain as part of the CSP system. We cut deadfall timber from the trails, thus eliminating patterns of detours that would develop.

The park's maintenance department brought in a wilderness trail expert for a weekend class at Sylvan Lake, and the class project was to redesign the trail encircling Sylvan Lake. Using our class project design, we accomplished that reconstruction, resurfacing that heavily used trail with crushed limestone to absorb the impact of many thousands of hikers. We relocated and reconstructed the one-hour horse trail near Blue Bell Lodge through contract provision in a timber sale; eliminated part of the trail through Cathedral Spires to reduce the number of access points to Harney Peak at the request of the USFS; turnpiked the very popular Trail #9 from Sylvan Lake to the Harney Peak Wilderness boundary and resisted pressures from the Forest Service to reduce use in the Black Elk Wilderness by registering hikers and enforcing a maximum quota. We relocated a one-mile section of Trail #4 from an unmaintainable draw bottom location to better suited hill sides, stretching the common convention of limiting slopes on trails from 10% to 20% to discourage hikers from cutting switchbacks.

Piece by piece we took control of the 60-mile trail system in the park. We did the maintenance, design, construction and elimination of the park's trail system in our efforts to make Custer State Park a better place to hike. People are fascinated by trails. Trails convey people to parts unknown and bring them nose to nose with the natural world. I am fascinated by trails too, especially the ones that lead to the backside of the mountain.

Winding things up

Over the years of first working for the SD Division of Forestry and then Custer State Park, I became familiar with Game Fish and Parks Commission meetings. The GF&P Commission is the citizens' overseeing board to Game Fish and Parks. In the early days when GF&P was housed in the Anderson Building; the Commission room was the scene of nearly all the meetings. Leather swivel chairs surrounded a big mahogany table, and the room filled with cigarette and cigar smoke as the commission conducted its business. One had to arrive early to get a seat by an open window or else suffer the consequence of all that blue haze. Usually, my part of the agenda was to periodically offer a report in which they were interested. Remodeling in the Anderson Building moved Game Fish and Parks to the Kneip Building and the Commission lost their legendary room. The park made a run to Pierre as the move was taking place and brought back the famous table which sits today in the basement of the office addition along with the swivel leather chairs.

The Commission began to meet in locations around the state, and in May of each year they met in the park. They usually met in the Blue Bell meeting room and would later party at Valhalla, a state-owned retreat facility for VIP's. We would prepare informational presentations on resource management activities, and occasionally I'd be responsible for a recreational excursion. Once I took the commissioners to a pond behind Valhalla where they enjoyed catching a number of oversize brook trout.

Commission members changed over the years; each usually served two 4- year terms. They were a likable bunch and took seriously their appointment by the governor. My last commission meeting was in May 2005. Dick Miller, the new director of the park, announced my retirement and read them my bio. The commissioners stood and gave me a round of applause. One anticipates what that final meeting might be like after thirty-one years.

On Dancing Here

My dance in this place has seemed like a dream
waltzing the systems to see the land shine,
releasing life's plenty on tree covered cline,
abundance displaying its primary theme.
Fire and smoke may seem kind of mean.
Winter flights try to elk numbers define.
Riders and auctions make park herds align
and dance to the landscape's edible green.
Springtime bison calves careen
cross flower strewn meadows amongst the pines.
Native grasses grace the scene
displaying nature's grand design.
The management team has sought to advance these
　　rhythms of Custer State Park's grand dance.

My Story, His Story
>(1971- Psalm 37:4. U of MN)
>"Come near to me, I have something to tell you;
>By songs long sung I will bring it about
>In a place of grass and morning dew.
>I will fulfill the desires of your heart
>With bison, forest, fire and drought.
>My fingers create my own work of art
>With sights so glorious your spirit will shout.
>You can learn how it all works together.
>And if you listen and do your part
>I'll enable you to weather
>The storms that come and the fires that start
>And those against you, seeking your end.
>I'll even throw in some saddle leather;
>Projects to plan, people to tend
>A season of fame to take to the heather,
>A time of renown, a team to lead."
>(2005- retirement from CSP to pastor The Little White Church)
>"Lean on me, your paths now I bend.
>Wait on me and learn to read
>The fresh change that to you I send.
>Serve my people and teach my word.
>Serve them all and meet their need;
>Learn to lead and cease to herd
>Those for whom I bled and for whom you'll bleed.
>Join me in seeing a cold heart turned."
>(2014- Lake Superior, Toftee, MN)
>"Hear me now for a season third.
>It's time to convey what you've learned long ago.
>Lessons you've gained are to be transferred
>To those you may not even know."

The Gray Light of Dawn

My trail's been in the gray light of dawn.
There are landmarks I have missed
In the morning fog and mist;
Things have seemed obscure, nearly gone.
The morning dew has soaked my boots,
I sometimes slip upon the roots.

But I persist and watch my feet,
Watching with the present light,
Walking on in spite of sight.
I labor making body heat.
Uphill, downhill, back and forth
Trying to keep track of north.

As I walk on some light breaks through
And beads of sweat form on my brow.
Path features are much plainer now
And other landmarks come in view.
As morning mists soon drift away
The better light displaces gray.

It's not for long, this long gray sliver
Of dawn that leads to the full day.
The trail goes quickly, mists drift away,
So by the time I reach the river
The sun has gained full power
And I cross over to the bright lit hour.

May you discern your trails, wherever they may lead you.

About the Author

Ron Walker worked in the Custer State Park from 1979-2005 as the Resource Program Manager, which included timber, range, wildlife, fire, and bison management. Through prose and poetry, much of it written prior to 2005, he offers a series of snapshots, an insider's view of what it was like to work with the precious natural resources of the park. You are invited to travel with him through the sights and sounds and smells of his experience. He trusts his own Park Song will strike a warm chord in your heart.

About JK Dooley

Paintings, fabric books and collages, pen and ink illustrations, beadwork and fiber projects compete for space in South Dakota artist JK Dooley's busy Black Hills studio.

Watercolor is JK's favorite way to create the cowboy and rodeo images for which she is known. A request from Ron Walker to help illustrate his upcoming book reignited an interest in pen and ink, for which she is most grateful.

Please visit *jkdooleyart.com* to view JK's portfolio.

Made in the USA
Middletown, DE
03 March 2024